FRESH WATER

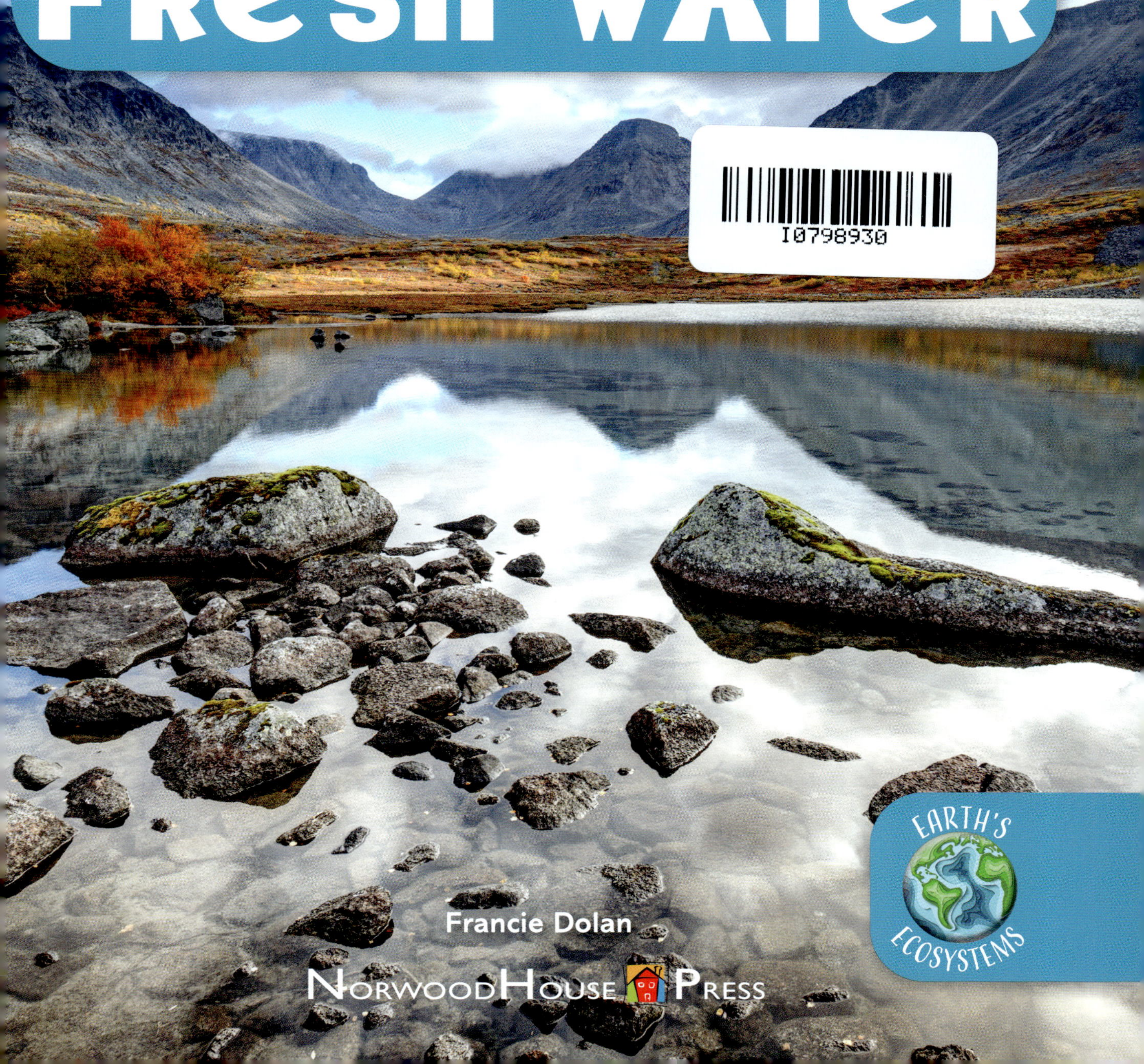

EARTH'S ECOSYSTEMS

Francie Dolan

NorwoodHouse Press

Cataloging-in-Publication Data

Names: Dolan, Francie.
Title: Fresh water / Francie Dolan.
Description: Buffalo, NY : Norwood House Press, 2026. | Series: Earth's ecosystems | Includes glossary and index.
Identifiers: ISBN 9781978577190 (pbk.) | ISBN 9781978577206 (library bound) | ISBN 9781978577213 (ebook)
Subjects: LCSH: Freshwater ecology--Juvenile literature.
Classification: LCC QH541.5.F7 D65 2026 | DDC 577.6--dc23

Published in 2026 by
Norwood House Press
2544 Clinton Street
Buffalo, NY 14224

Designer: Rhea Magaro
Editor: Kim Thompson

Photo credits: Cover, p. 1 Gregory A. Pozhvanov, Kumer Oksa-na/Shutterstock.com; p. 3 Me dia/Shutterstock.com; p. 5 Maksim Safaniuk/Shutterstock.com; p. 6 Photoongraphy/Shutterstock.com; p. 7 Noko Cloud/Shutterstock.com; p. 9 Julija Vidjajeva/Shutterstock.com; p. 10 AlinaMD/Shutterstock.com; p. 12 Damsea/Shutterstock.com; p. 13 Dudarev Mikhail/Shutterstock.com; p. 15 dailymotor/Shutterstock.com; p. 16 Martin Fowler/Shutterstock.com; p. 18 Aleron Val/Shutterstock.com; p. 19 Cami Johnson/Shutterstock.com; p. 21 Al Carrera/Shutterstock.com

Printed in the United States of America

CPSIA compliance information: Batch #CWNHP26: For further information contact Norwood House Press at 1-800-237-9932.

TABLE OF CONTENTS

The Freshwater Ecosystem

Eco- means "home" or "environment." *System* means "a group of things that work together." Earth has many **ecosystems** that support life. Each is home to a network of living things that depend on each other.

One kind of ecosystem is a freshwater ecosystem. Fresh water is found in streams, rivers, ponds, and lakes. It is a precious resource. More than 100,000 **species**, including humans, need fresh water to survive.

Most of Earth's water is salt water found in oceans. Just three percent is fresh water.

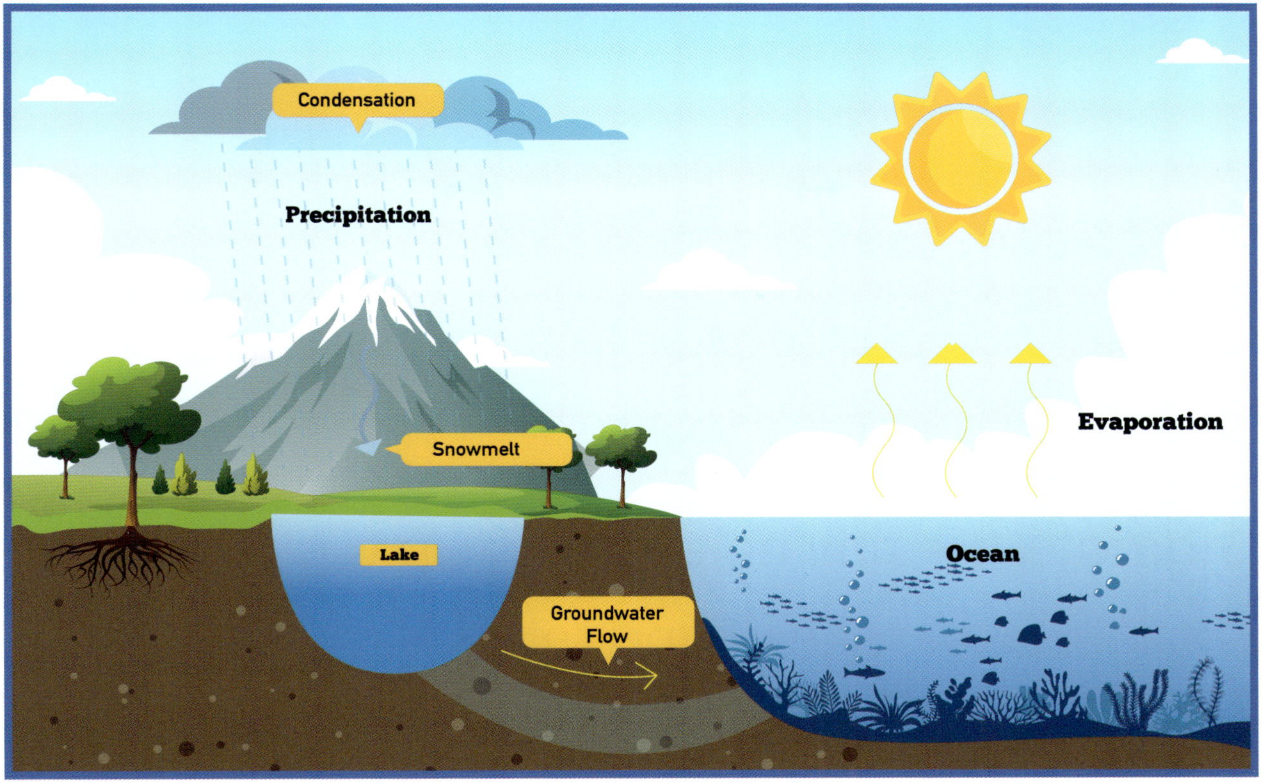

During the water cycle, water **evaporates** from bodies of water, including oceans. As water vapor rises, it leaves behind salt and other impurities. It becomes "fresh."

Freshwater Plants

Special **adaptations** help freshwater plants survive in a watery world.

Stomata are tiny holes that help a plant "breathe," or take in and release gases from the air. Most plants have stomata on the underside of their leaves. Not water lilies! Their stomata are found on the tops of leaves that float on the surface of the water.

A cattail's strong roots anchor it to the bottom of a pond or lake. Its leaves reach above the water to get sunlight. Long, stiff, hollow stems help cattails stand straight up in the water.

Freshwater Animals

Many animals have adapted to live in freshwater ecosystems.

Gills allow fish to breathe **oxygen** from the water. Scales protect their bodies from water just like shingles protect a roof. Some fish have swim bladders that fill with air to help them float.

Beavers have dense, waterproof fur. Their eyes, ears, and nose are high on the head so that they stay above water. Webbed feet help beavers swim. Sharp teeth help them cut plants that are used to build lodges and **dams**.

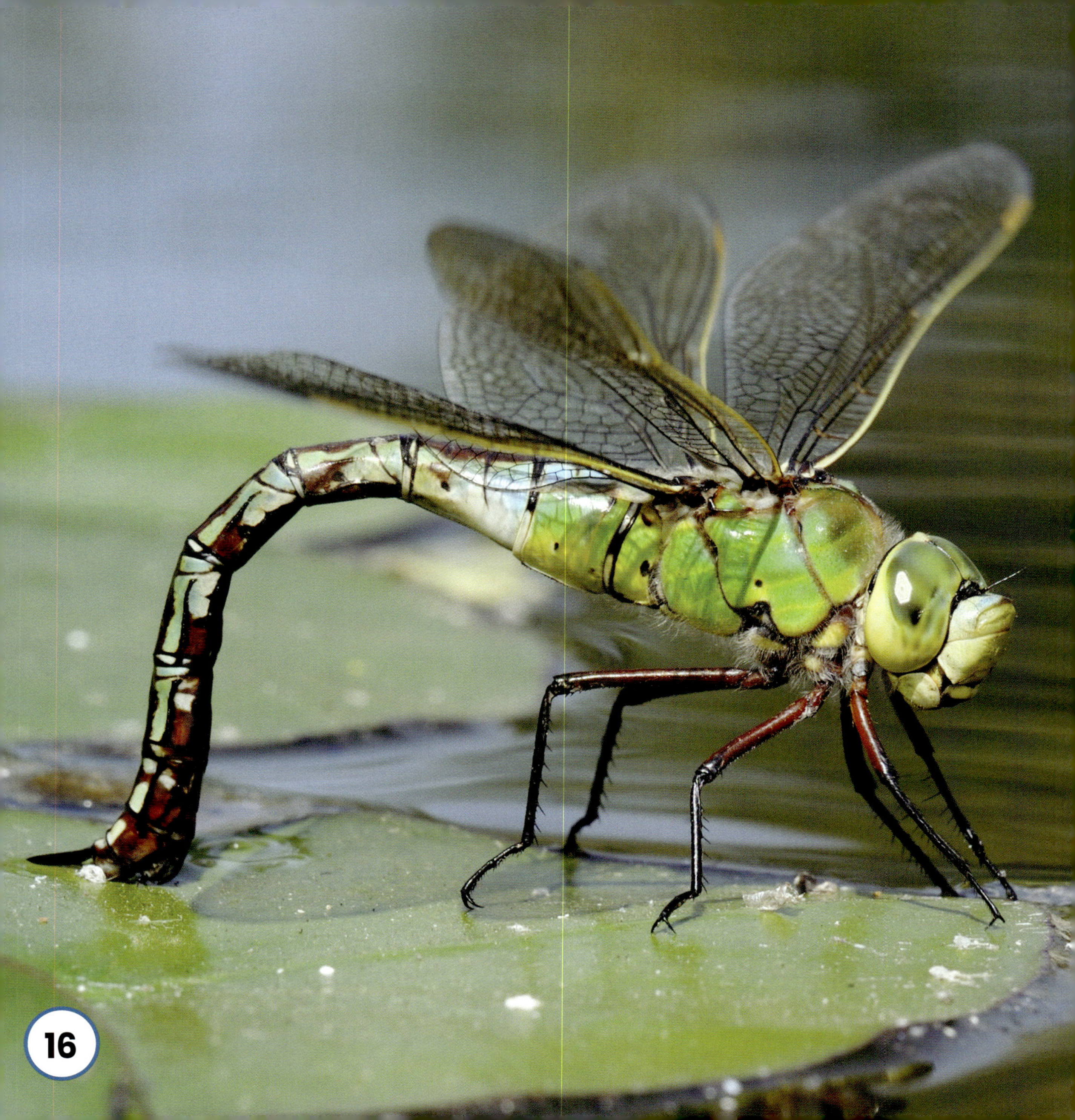

Dragonflies spend part of their lives in water and part on land. **Nymphs** hatch in the water, where they can swim to find food. Adult dragonflies have wings. This lets them fly to new places to lay eggs.

Freshwater Food Chains

In fresh water, living things eat other living things in food chains. A water beetle might eat algae. A bluegill may swallow the beetle.

A river otter might eat the bluegill. After the otter dies, its body may sink to the bottom of the river. **Bacteria** will help it **decompose**.

All living things in freshwater ecosystems depend on each other for survival. These places are important for plants, animals, and planet Earth.

Glossary

adaptations (ad-ap-TAY-shuhns): physical or behavioral changes that help plants and animals survive in their environment

bacteria (bak-TEER-ee-uh): microscopic, single-celled living things

dams (dams): barriers built across streams and rivers to hold back the flow of water and create water reserves

decompose (dee-kuhm-POZE): to rot or decay and return nutrients to the soil

ecosystems (EE-koh-sis-tuhms): natural communities where plants, animals, and their environment all work together

evaporates (i-VAP-uh-rates): changes from a liquid into a vapor or gas and rises into the air

gills (gilz): pairs of organs near a fish's mouth through which it breathes by extracting oxygen from water

nymphs (nimfs): young forms of insects that change into adults by shedding their skin many times

oxygen (AHK-si-juhn): a gas with no color that humans and animals need to breathe

species (SPEE-sheez): a group of living things that are alike and can reproduce together

Thinking Questions

1. What is an ecosystem?
2. Why is fresh water a precious resource?
3. Give an example of an adaptation that helps freshwater plants survive.
4. Give an example of an adaptation that helps freshwater animals survive.
5. What does a food chain show?

Index

About the Author

Francie Dolan is continually amazed by the natural world and how Earth's plants, animals, and natural resources are interconnected. From her home near Seattle, Washington, she loves to hike and explore forests, lakes, mountains, and the seashore. When she gets home, she likes to draw and write about what she sees on her adventures.